Banff & Jasper

National Parks

A Pictorial Guide to the Spectacular
World Heritage Sites of Banff & Jasper National Parks

The National Parks concept originates in North America and is barely a century old. Banff and Jasper National Parks are fine examples of how valuable and practical the concept has proved to be.

Natural ecosystems of eternal beauty exist in a pristine state - protected forever - allowing their fragile web of life to continue undisturbed.

The spectacular scenery shown here, in large format photography, should remind us all what tremendous treasures the Parks are - and make us realize the need to protect them forever. Do your part.

Text and photographs by
GEORGE BRYBYCIN

GB PUBLISHING

Common Harebell (Campanula rotundifolia)

Banff National Park

Banff National Park is the most famous of the Rocky Mountain National Parks.

In 1885, hot sulfuric springs were discovered near the current site of the town of Banff. Recognizing the importance of the place, a small nature preserve was created to protect the area - and has been enlarged several times since then.

In 1930, The National Parks Act was passed and the Park was enlarged to its present size - 6,641 square kilometers. God bless the wisdom of our forefathers.

The area became easily accessible when the Canadian Pacific Railway, in its push west, reached Banff in 1883. Five years later, the first tourist accommodation, The Banff Springs Hotel, opened its doors to the public.

The Park and town of Banff were named after the Scottish birthplace of Lord Strathcona, who was then director of the CPR.

A road to Lake Louise was built in 1920, which later became part of the Trans-Canada Highway, reaching the Rogers Pass in 1962.

The Rocky Mountains were formed from very old sedimentary rock when the shallow seas that covered most of the area, dried up causing cracking, shifting and faulting of the surface. Enormous internal forces and pressure broke open the weakened Earth's crust, lifting the entire region upwards along these faults, forming the base of the Rockies about 75 million years ago.

Many more powerful tectonic events took place during that time, reshaping and lifting the Rockies to new heights. During several Ice Ages, the Rockies were carved and reshaped time and again - leaving new, deep valleys and lakes after the ice had melted away. The emerald Lake Louise is one of the most famous.

It was only 10,000 years ago that the Wisconsin Glaciation took place - smothering the Rockies and most of Canada with a huge layer of ice.

The Great Continental Divide causes the water from melting ice and snow to flow west to the Pacific Ocean, north to the Arctic Ocean and east to the Atlantic.

The Rockies are home to a rich and diversified flora and fauna and, regardless of global warming caused by global overdevelopment and overpopulation, are still in relatively healthy condition - mostly due to their protective National Park status.

We must remember that the National Parks Act of 1930 clearly stipulates that Parks must be left unimpaired for the enjoyment of future generations. The Parks must remain pristine, unimpaired, natural.

An invigorating hike from Moraine Lake, up to Larch Valley, rewards one with a splendid view of Larch groves
and a magnificent panorama of The Valley of the Ten Peaks. Late autumn, when the
needles of the Larch turn gold, is the most enjoyable time to visit.

Banff's principal landmark, Mt. Rundle (2998m), is named after Methodist missionary Robert T. Rundle, who first sighted the mountain in 1847. It is easily accessible by the west slopes but may present a major climbing challenge from the northeast. A mixed forest, in its autumn glory, is in the foreground.

Three feet of snow by Peyto Lake, in late autumn, makes access a bit difficult. The hiker here has sunk to well above his knees
in the white fluff but truly enjoys this splendid winter wonderland. On the left is Caldron Peak (2917m);
on the right are the Mistaya River Valley and Waterfowl Lakes.

An early winter morning at the spectacular Lake Louise. Named after Queen Victoria's daughter, Princess Louise, in 1884. It is a deep glacial lake with turquoise green waters and truly alpine surroundings. The long, snowy ridge is Mt. Victoria (3464m), on the right – pointy Mt. Whyte (2983m); both present a certain climbing challenge.

Just west of Banff townsite, three Vermilion Lakes are located along the Bow River. The area is home to a richly diversified wildlife. Although human excess eliminated the moose 15 years ago, elk, deer, coyote, bear and the occasional wolf still frequent the area. Beaver, muskrat, scores of waterfowl, bald eagle and osprey call it home.

This view of the right flank of the great Moraine Lake highlights the glacial green waters and the alpine paradise enjoyed by canoeist,
hiker and tourist alike. The Tower of Babel (2360m) guards the lake and this small quartzite hump
is a very attractive climbing site of various challenges.

For some, there is nothing more fascinating than high mountain vistas. Here is a morning view of the Bow River Valley surrounded by
high mountains – from Mt. Lefroy on the left, to Mt. Stephen on the far right. The Bow River meanders through
the valley and on the right is the Waputik Range. Photographed from Mt. Hector (3394m).

The spectacular, turquoise Hector Lake is located at the east end of the Wapta Icefield, it provides silt which creates the emerald colour of the water. The colour varies from turquoise, to dark green, to blue - depending on the time of year, day, direction of the light and the intensity of the glacial meltwater.

In the Hawaiian Islands rainbows are almost a daily occurrence. In the Rockies they are far more rare – especially a double rainbow. This photo was taken by Bow Falls on the Bow River as a ribbon of vivid colours adorns Mt. Rundle on a rainy July afternoon. An old cliché comes to mind: be in the right place, at the right time and one gets a great shot.

East of Lake Louise, along the Bow River, a freight train "puffs" its way east – bringing goods from the port of Vancouver to eastern markets. Low morning light, mysterious clouds and mountains create the very special ambience, which this photo conveys beautifully.

The winter wonderland along the Icefields Parkway. Snowfall has turned an ordinary forest into a great white paradise.
In the center stands magnificent Mt. Erasmus (3265m), named after Peter Erasmus,
a guide and interpreter with the Palliser Expedition.

East of the Columbia Icefield, by the forks of the North Saskatchewan and Alexandra Rivers, looms monumental Mt. Amery (3329m).
First climbed in 1929 by L.S. Amery and B. Meredith, guided by E. Fuez Jr.   It required a major climbing effort due to
its height and topography. The ascent took 11 hours, which included fording the river.

Canoeing is as Canadian as maple syrup or hockey. These two water sports enthusiasts set out on the Bow River, in Banff,
for a nice autumn voyage to Canmore. On the left is rocky Tunnel Mountain, and in the distance,
the snow-clad Fairholme Range shines in the morning sun.

Moraine Lake does not need much of an introduction – this world-renowned jewel is as beautiful as ever. How did the lake come to be? Geologists speculate that a large rockslide fell from Mt. Babel and dammed the creek. Others say that a pile of rocks fell on a glacier in the upper valley and traveled, piggyback, on the glacier until it melted down in its present location.

As with most of the lakes in the Rockies, Lower Waterfowl Lake is glacier fed – thus that marvelous green water. The Wapta Icefield, Peyto
Glacier and a number of small, hanging glaciers provide silty water via the Mistaya River. Lush vegetation, flowers and
forests surround the lake – providing a suitable habitat for many mammals and waterfowl.

The fabulous, world famous Lake Louise, with landscaped gardens in the front of the Chateau and these high, glaciated mountains all around. In the middle background stands monumental Mt. Victoria (3464m). Imagine how different a scene this was for early explorer and guide, Tom Wilson, when he first visited the lake in 1882. It must have been a wild, pristine, beautiful sight.

A few hundred cross-country skiers race for fame, glory and healthy exercise in an annual event staged at Lake Louise. Lofty Mt. Victoria (3464m) stands nearby, as if cheering the noble efforts of the athletes. Would you join the race? It is healthy and fun, and builds character.

For thousands of years, the Eskimo people lived in igloos. Today the average Inuit probably wouldn't know how to build one. They live in comfortable houses with indoor plumbing. Now, skiers and winter campers build the occasional snow hut for the fun of it. Actually, igloos are warmer than tents and do not make any noise on windy nights, as tents do. Pilot Mountain (2935m) provides the background.

A glacier carved this little valley just southeast of Moraine Lake, Consolation Valley houses the two Consolation Lakes. This beautiful, hidden valley is flanked by Panorama Ridge to the east, Mt. Quadra to the south and Mt. Babel to the west. Golden Larches are beautiful in the autumn, but the Grizzly Bears, who frequent the area, are unpredictable. Caution is advised.

The most celebrated lake of the Rockies is Lake Louise. It has all the ingredients: emerald glacial waters, lush vegetation and challenging glacier-clad mountains. For the most part, however, the Chateau is behind its fame – a world-class hotel with all the services and amenities necessary for a great holiday.

Shrubs, small trees, alpine plants – this is an alpine tundra in the Columbia Icefield area – the upper limit of vegetation – life. It is, however, beautiful in its autumn colours. Desolate Mt. Athabasca dominates the skyline as it awaits the inevitable coming of winter - when life seems to disappear for up to seven months.

Yet another emerald jewel, Bow Lake, located east of the Bow Summit, along the Icefields Parkway. It is a large lake, whose waters come from the Wapta Icefield located south of the lake. Bow Glacier gives birth to the Bow River, which meanders east towards the Prairies and then to the Hudson Bay and the Atlantic Ocean.

Photographed at nearly full moon, Herbert Lake seems to be in daylight. Faint star trails in a slightly hazy sky remind us that it is,
indeed, night. The lake is located a few minutes drive northwest of Lake Louise. The mountains seen
here are Mt. Temple and the Mt. Victoria Groups.

Is that a mirror, or Two Jack Lake? Actually, it's both. A gorgeous sunrise lights the less known northeast face
of Mt. Rundle (2998m), near Banff. Very seldom do all the elements come together
for a great photo: clear sky, bright sunlight and no winds.

Elk or Wapiti (Cervus canadensis) of the Cervidae Family, is a large mammal of the Deer Family, which once inhabited the entire
north of the continent. Today, it is confined to the Rockies and northwestern mountains. Elk are browsers
and consume a great variety of foods – about 20 kilograms per day.

The Moose (Alces alces) is the world's largest deer and is found in northwestern North America and Eurasia. It is a browser but feeds mainly on aquatic vegetation in the summer. An adult bull may weigh up to 750 kilograms - a cow may exceed 500. A Moose's appetite is prodigious – it may consume 30 kilograms of food a day.

A tourist view of Mt. Babel (3101m) in the Valley of the Ten Peaks near Moraine Lake. The mountain was first ascended
by A.R. Hart, E.O. Wheeler, L.C. Wilson and H.H. Worsfold in 1910 and is flanked by Mt. Quadra
on the left, and Mountains Little and Bowlen on the right.

The picturesque Mt. Amery (3329m) reflects its north face in a tundra pond. The mountain is high and glaciated and difficult to climb.
In addition, one must ford the wide North Saskatchewan River, whose water level can be very high in summer.
Needless to say, the water comes from glaciers and is very cold.

Jasper National Park

Jasper National Park is the largest and most pristine in the Rockies. Established in 1907, it protects 10,878 square kilometers of spectacular wilderness and is only slightly smaller than the island of Jamaica. In Canada, Jasper park is second in size only to Wood Buffalo National Park.

The park is named for Jasper Hawes, a well-known trader with the North West Company, who established a trading post, just east of today's Jasper townsite, in 1812. The post was a trading and resting-place for early explorers, traders, missionaries and, later, mountaineers, geologists and adventurers. The area was opened to all when a railway line was built in 1911, and the Canadian National Railway constructed the town of Jasper and the Jasper Park Lodge, just east of town, to accommodate curious tourists, gold seekers and fur traders.

Because of friendly topography and a relatively low elevation of just 1131 meters, Yellowhead Pass made it easy to build both a railway line and a road to link Jasper with British Columbia and open up tourist travel.

One of the world's most spectacular scenic roads, from Lake Louise to Jasper, was completed in 1940. The route is now a "must-see" for all Rocky Mountain visitors.

Large, crystalline rivers like the Sunwapta and the Athabasca meander along the Icefields Parkway. In the southeastern corner of the Park, the magnificent Columbia Icefield is nestled amongst jagged high peaks. At 325 square kilometers, it is the largest body of ancient ice in the Rockies.

Several major ice tongues, or glaciers, descend from the icefield - two of them, the Athabasca and Dome Glaciers, can be seen from the highway and the largest of them, the Saskatchewan Glacier, can be viewed after a short hike to Parker's Ridge.

The Park's largest and most beautiful lake, Maligne Lake, does not deserve the name. It originates from the treacherous waters at the lower end of the Maligne River.

Many wonder at the colour of the mountain rivers and lakes - asking where these emerald-green hues come from.

Rock flour, or powdered rock, is blown by the wind over all the glaciers and is carried by their meltwaters to the various rivers and lakes, where it hangs suspended in the icy waters. The direction and intensity of sunlight, reflected of the powdered rock, creates the varying spectacle of colour.

A brief geological history of how the Rockies came to be, can be found on page 3.

As is the case with all National Parks, Jasper National Park protects a huge, spectacular, pristine wilderness. Very few explorers have penetrated some areas of the Park. Even today, there are a number of unclimbed peaks - places that Eagles, Grizzly Bears and Caribou call home.

The National Parks Act of 1930 stipulates that the role of National Parks is to protect these pristine areas and leave them undamaged and undisturbed for the enjoyment of future generations.

Let's make sure it stays that way.

Jasper Park's prime tourist attraction, and a beautiful sight, is Maligne Lake. This glacial lake is 22 km long, and its vicinity is permanent home for Moose, Grizzly Bears, a few smaller mammals and a great variety of waterfowl. Many wonder how such a beautiful place got such an ominous name. The name was first given to the treacherous lower end of the Maligne River.

The rugged ridge of the Queen Elizabeth Range flanks Medicine Lake on the north side. The lake is a unique phenomenon. In late autumn,
the meltwaters stop flowing into the lake and underground channels drain the water. The result is an empty lake for the winter.
In the spring, when the snow and glaciers around Maligne Lake begin melting, the lake fills up for the summer.

Gravel, silt and clay are the "soil" of the Athabasca Glacier moraines. That soil barely supports the alpine Willow Herb and a few other flowers and plants. Summer and this plant life lasts barely four months here, before it returns to a state of snow, ice and violent blizzards. In the background are glacier-clad Mt. Athabasca and Mt. Andromeda.

Peaceful Patricia Lake is located just a short drive from Jasper townsite. Autumn leaves its mark on poplar trees and the air is cooler than
the water, creating a morning mist. Pyramid Mountain (2766m,) with a microwave communication facility
on its summit, reflects its rugged east face in calm morning waters.

Picturesque Patricia Lake, just north of Jasper townsite, is well worth visiting. Take time to stroll along the shore. Waterfowl make
their summer home here. Osprey can be seen fishing - moose browse along the shore. The view is
to the southwest and features peaks southwest of Jasper.

A man in the loneliness of the vast, pristine wilderness. A hiker enjoys the sweeping vista of the Queen Elizabeth and Colin Ranges from the vantage point (2790m) just east of Opal Peak, north of Maligne Lake. On the way here, the fortunate may catch a glimpse of the Mountain Caribou, while the unfortunate might encounter a Grizzly Bear.

An invigorating hike from Pyramid Lake, north of Jasper, gets one to the back of Pyramid Mountain (2766m). Then a not-too-difficult scramble on good rock gets one to the summit. A huge microwave station occupies the entire summit. From here, sweeping views can be enjoyed in all directions. This photo features the view to the west, towards the Victoria Cross Ranges. A sharp eye will spot the pointy Mt. Robson on the right horizon.

Dome Glacier is one of about six major ice tongues coming down from the Columbia Icefield. Flanked by Snow Dome (3456m) on the left, and Mt. Kitchener (3505m) on the right. The glacier is seldom used to access the Icefield because of hidden crevasses and a steep grade. The Athabasca Glacier is commonly used for Icefield trips.

Northwest of the Columbia Icefield, along Sunwapta River on old river's channel, canoe enthusiasts find a serene moment at sundown.
On the wide river's flats, a suitable environment exists for Mountain Caribou, which spend their winters here,
migrating to higher valleys for the summer — escaping the menacing bugs and wolves.

14 km, or so, up Maligne Lake, the famed Spirit Island – which is actually a peninsula – is found. From here, people take canoe trips to the far end
of the lake, where the campground at Coronet Creek allows further exploration. The Brazeau Icefield is just around the corner.
It is a paradise of the first magnitude – a "must-see" for the true explorer.

Mt. Edith Cavell (3363m), is a lofty landmark seen from Jasper and vicinity and was first ascended in 1915 by A.J. Gilmour and E. Holway. Several challenging routes, including the renowned north face, lead to the summit. This photo features Cavell's main ice-clad peak on the left and its west subsidiary peak on the right, reflected in crystal clear Cavell Lake.

Viewed from the Icefields Parkway, Mushroom Peak (3200m) presents an interesting silhouette. It is readily accessible after fording the icy waters of the Sunwapta River and negotiating its north glacier. Once on the summit, one is likely to see elusive and famous mountains like: Diadem, Woolley, The Twins, Alberta and scores of others. It was first climbed solo by N.E. Odell in 1947.

The beautiful, broad Sunwapta River Valley, just northwest of the Columbia Icefield, photographed on an autumn morning. The valley is
the winter home for a small herd of Mountain Caribou who migrate to high valleys for the summer.
The icy sentinel, Mt. Kitchener (3505m), stands guard at the center.

The grand panorama viewed from the summit of Mt. Athabasca (3490m). On the left stands Mt. Andromeda; in the center, on the horizon, is the second-highest elevation in the Rockies – Mt. Columbia (3747m); and on the right, are the south slopes of the Snow Dome. Notice two climbers approaching the summit ridge on the right. First ascended by prominent early explorers J.N. Collie and H. Woolley in 1898.

Descending the north icefield of Mt. Athabasca (3490m) after a successful summit climb. Treading between large crevasses and hanging blocks of ice, this simple climb could turn into a very scary business at any time. This photo clearly illustrates what happens when a glacier rolls over a steep rocky hump – it cracks, breaks, crumbles, separates and falls. Glaciers are very dangerous places to visit.

There are never too many photos of Maligne Lake. This is Leah Peak (2801m), photographed in low sunset light, and the unusually calm lake. On the right is Samson Peak (3081m). The peaks were first climbed in 1926 and 1928, respectively.

The north end of Colin Range, along the Athabasca River, northeast of Jasper. The peaks of the Colin Range aren't high, but can be quite challenging. Mt. Colin (2687m) (not in photo) is a dominant elevation and presents a considerable challenge for climbers. Access is difficult because it involves fording the icy Athabasca River.

A gorgeous autumn day along the Athabasca River, southeast of Jasper. Some of the easily recognizable mountains are: from the left, Mt. Kerkeslin, Dragon Peak, Mt. Christie, and Brussels Peak. The top of Mt. Fryatt is visible on the right.

A classic view of Mt. Athabasca, Mt. Andromeda and the Athabasca Glacier viewed from the slopes of Wilcox Mountain.
One can see clearly just how quickly the glacier melts, perhaps 15 meters per year – the same as most
glaciers in the Northern Hemisphere. Global warming, too much pollution or both?

No, this is not an aerial photo. The author sweated it all the way to the summit of Pyramid Mountain (2766m) to photograph Pyramid Lake, just north of Jasper. It was a pleasant climb on a gorgeous autumn day. The views from here are surprisingly great in every direction – even Mt. Robson can be seen.

This cow Moose (Alces alces), and her calf, browsed in the bush along the Maligne River for a long while – frustrating five professional photographers who linger nearby. Then, suddenly, the moose decide to cross the river – to everyone's delight. Way to go, Moosee!

The amazing Maligne Lake as viewed from a vantage point (2790m) north of Opal Hills. The incredible vistas to the south
feature endless mountains, forests and the great turquoise waters of Maligne Lake. The woods in the
right foreground are home to a healthy colony of moose year-round.

This is the lofty world of a sea of peaks, viewed from Sunwapta Peak (3315m) in early morning light. Located across the valley north
of the Columbia Icefield, it is an easy but very toilsome climb. In 1906, J. Simpson was first to climb Sunwapta Peak solo.
The author has climbed this interesting peak twice, also solo. The view here is to the east.

The Author's Thoughts

In order to publish twenty-nine books, mostly on the subject of the Rocky Mountains, one must love these mountains deeply, work hard and be persistent and prolific. George has no life other than the mountain life. You will never see him in smoky, noisy bars. He dresses casually and lives a very simple, humble life. He is a totally non-materialistic chap who is happy with very little he owns: deriving his inspiration and strength from nature and the beauty of the mountains.

George does not have a black belt in shopping. Possessions won't make me happy, he says. Sooner or later, all those knick-knacks people horde so religiously, will wind up in the garbage, polluting and poisoning us all.

So, George does not go on mindless shopping sprees. When he has saved enough money, he publishes another book filled with beauty and advice on how to preserve it; or he donates the money to plant trees. Thanks to George's wisdom and generosity, 1,100 new trees have been planted in Calgary, to date. Wouldn't it be wise to plant trees around the area where you live – to live in an urban forest, rather than an concrete jungle?

George's first contact with nature came when, at the age of seven, he joined the Boy Scouts. The desire to reach the mountain tops came soon after, and to date, he has ascended close to four hundred mountains. Later in life, he traveled the world and learned a great deal.

In time, he became very much aware of the effect six billion people have on the environment just by existing; not to mention the endless development – huge new projects for fun and profit. We must hurry, hurry, to consume more, more! Or else? We run the risk of becoming a decent, reasonable and normal people.

It is very easy to realize that our green lands shrink in direct proportion to the population explosion. "Truly, says George, I would not want to be around when the population reaches fifteen or twenty billion!" Even penguins wouldn't tolerate this kind of density. We are supposed to be able to think rationally, yet the growth of some nations is totally out of control. While rich, developed countries have a low growth rate, the poorer countries double their population every twenty-five years, or so – digging graves for themselves. Poor families cannot afford to feed and educate one or two children, but they have six? What will their future be? Miserable, hopeless poverty.

"I have no power to implement any solution, but I know the outcome," says George. "It will more closely resemble Hell than Heaven."

"We cannot avoid the oncoming catastrophe, we can only postpone it a little. How? By trying to reduce population growth and not supporting economic growth simply for growth's sake. Do not buy any disposable items; do not buy over-packaged, half-empty boxes. Demand a more environmentally responsible approach to marketing from stores and manufacturers. Be rational. Think about what you buy, and why. Do you really need it all? Explain to your children that the senseless buying of any junk is a crime against the environment and must not be tolerated any longer.

As you turn the pages of this edition and admire the paradise it presents, ask yourself if you want these beautiful places to last.

Front cover: Larch Valley, Banff National Park
Back cover: Maligne Lake, Jasper National Park

Design: George Brybycin
Typeset: K & H United Co.
Created & produced in Canada
Printed in China by Everbest Printing Co.

ISBN 0-919029-28-0

For current list, please write to:
GB PUBLISHING, Box 6292, Station D,
Calgary, Alberta Canada T2P 2C9

Photographic studies by George Brybycin :

The High Rockies, Colourful Calgary, Our Fragile Wilderness, The Rocky Mountains, Banff National Park, Jasper National Park, Colourful Calgary II, Wildlife in the Rockies, Rocky Mountain Symphony, Enchanted Wilderness, Wilderness Odyssey, Rocky Mountain Symphony II, Romance of the Rockies, Calgary - The Sunshine City, The Living Rockies, Cosmopolitan Calgary, Banff and Jasper N.P., The Rockies: Wildlife, The Majestic Rockies, Emerald Waters of the Rockies, The Canadian Rockies Panoramas, Eternal Rockies, Calgary, the Stampede City and Environs, Alpine Meadows, The Rockies - British Columbia - The North, Rocky Mountain Odyssey, Banff & Jasper National Parks II, The Canadian Rocky, The Canadian Rockies Panoromas II.

George Brybycin's collection of 20,000 35mm colour slides is FOR SALE.

Subjects include: The Rockies, Western and Northern Canada, Calgary, The 1988 Olympics, Alaska, The Western U.S. and the World. Also available is the collection of all 29 George's books. Offers may be tendered to GB Publishing at the address above.